First World War
and Army of Occupation
War Diary
France, Belgium and Germany

66 DIVISION
197 Infantry Brigade,
Brigade Trench Mortar Battery
24 February 1914 - 27 September 1918

WO95/3137/4

The Naval & Military Press Ltd
www.nmarchive.com
Published in association with The National Archives

Published by

The Naval & Military Press Ltd

Unit 10 Ridgewood Industrial Park,

Uckfield, East Sussex,

TN22 5QE England

Tel: +44 (0) 1825 749494

www.naval-military-press.com

www.nmarchive.com

This diary has been reprinted in facsimile from the original. Any imperfections are inevitably reproduced and the quality may fall short of modern type and cartographic standards.

© **Crown Copyright**
Images reproduced by permission of The National Archives, London, England, 2015.

Contents

Document type	Place/Title	Date From	Date To
Heading	WO95/3137/4		
Heading	6th Division 197th Infy Bde Lt Trench Mortar Feb 1917-Sep 1918 Missing 1918 Mar To Aug		
Heading	197th Brigade 66th Division Disembarked Havre 27.2.17.		
War Diary	Havre	24/02/1914	28/02/1914
Heading	197th Brigade 66th 1 Division. 197th Light Mortar Battery March 1917.		
War Diary	Thiennes	01/03/1917	01/03/1917
War Diary	Boeseghem	01/03/1917	07/03/1917
War Diary	Locan	04/03/1917	09/03/1917
War Diary	Bethune	09/03/1917	09/03/1917
War Diary	Gorre	14/03/1917	31/03/1917
Heading	19th Brigade. 66th Division 197th Light Trench Mortar Battery April 1917.		
War Diary	Gorre	01/04/1917	30/04/1917
Miscellaneous	3rd Echelon Base	01/05/1917	01/05/1917
Heading	197th Brigade 66th Division 197th Light Trench Mortar Battery May 1917.		
War Diary	Gorre	01/05/1917	31/05/1917
Miscellaneous	DAG 3rd Echelon	31/05/1917	31/05/1917
Heading	197th Brigade 66th Division 197th Light Trench Mortar Battery June 1917.		
War Diary	Gorre	01/06/1917	21/06/1917
War Diary	Bellerive	22/06/1917	30/06/1917
Heading	197th Brigade. 66th Division. 197th Light Trench Mortar Battery July 1917.		
Heading	War Diary of 197th. Light Trench Mortar Battery. From 1st. July 1917 To 31st. July 1917 To 31st. July 1917. Volume 6.		
War Diary	Couder Kerque Branch	01/07/1914	09/07/1914
War Diary	Zuidcoote	10/07/1917	12/07/1917
War Diary	Coxyde-Les-Bains	13/04/1917	16/04/1917
War Diary	Oost-Dunkerque	17/07/1917	30/07/1917
War Diary	Coxyde	31/07/1917	31/07/1917
Heading	197th Brigade 66th Division 197th Light Trench Mortar Battery August 1917.		
Heading	War Diary Of 197th Light Trench Mortar Battery. Form 1-8-17 Of 31-8-17 Volume VII		
War Diary	Coxyde Bains	01/08/1914	20/08/1914
War Diary	Oost Dunkerque	21/08/1917	31/08/1917
Heading	197th Brigade 66th Division 197th Light Trench Mortar Battery September 1917.		
Heading	War Diary of 197th. Light Trench Mortar Battery. From:- 1st. September 1917. To:- 30th. September 1917. Volume 8		
War Diary	Coxyde Bains	01/08/1914	24/09/1914
War Diary	Bray Dunes	25/09/1917	27/09/1917
War Diary	Arques	28/09/1917	30/09/1917

Heading	197th Brigade 66th Division 197th Light Mortar Battery October 1917		
War Diary	Arques	01/10/1917	02/10/1917
War Diary	Eecke	03/10/1917	04/10/1917
War Diary	Winnezeele	05/10/1917	05/10/1917
War Diary	Ypres	05/10/1917	11/10/1917
War Diary	Winnezeele	12/10/1917	20/10/1917
War Diary	Renescure	21/10/1917	31/10/1917
Heading	197th Brigade 66th Division 197th Light Trench Mortar Battery November 1917.		
Heading	War Diary of 197th Light Trench Mortar Battery From 1-11-17 To 30-11-17 Volume X		
War Diary	Renescure	01/11/1917	08/11/1917
War Diary	Westoutre	09/11/1917	09/11/1917
War Diary	Ypres	10/11/1917	10/11/1917
War Diary	Zonebeke (Sector)	11/11/1917	19/11/1917
War Diary	Ypres	20/11/1917	20/11/1917
War Diary	Dickebush	21/11/1917	22/11/1917
War Diary	Staple	23/11/1917	30/11/1917
Heading	197th Brigade 66th Division 197th Light Trench Battery December 1917.		
Heading	War Diary of 197th Light Trench Mortar Battery From 1-12-17 To 31-12-17 Volume XI		
War Diary	Staple	01/12/1917	31/12/1917
Heading	197th L.b Brigade Trench Mortar Jan 1918		
War Diary	Staple	01/01/1918	10/01/1918
War Diary	Morbecque	11/01/1918	14/01/1918
War Diary	Halifax	15/01/1918	16/01/1918
War Diary	Ypres	17/01/1918	17/01/1918
War Diary	Halifax Area	28/01/1918	02/02/1918
War Diary	Yypres	03/02/1918	08/02/1918
War Diary	Halifax Area	09/02/1918	09/02/1918
War Diary	St Janter Bazien	10/02/1918	15/02/1918
War Diary	Marcelcave	16/02/1918	27/02/1918
War Diary	Villers Carbonnel	28/02/1918	28/02/1918
Heading	War Diary of 197th L.T.M. Battery From Feb 1st To Feb 28th 1918		
Heading	War Diary of 197th L.T.M. Battery From 1st September 1918 To 30th September 1918		
War Diary	Berneval-Le-Grand	01/09/1918	10/09/1918
War Diary	Abancourt	18/09/1918	18/09/1918
War Diary	Haudricourt	19/09/1918	27/09/1918

No 95/3137/4

66TH DIVISION
197TH INFY BDE

LT TRENCH MORTAR BTY
FEB 1917–SEP 1918

MISSING 1918 MAR TO AUG

197th Brigade.

66th Division.

Disembarked Havre 27.2.17.

197th LIGHT TRENCH MORTAR BATTERY FEBRUARY 1917.

Confidential   Army Form C. 2118.

Volume I
WAR DIARY
of 197 Light Trench Mortar Battery.

INTELLIGENCE SUMMARY.
(Erase heading not required.) From 27/1/17 to 28/3/17.

Place	Date	Hour	Summary of Events and Information	Remarks and references to Appendices
Havre	27/3/17	12.30 pm	Disembarked at Havre. Marched to & stayed at No 2 Rest Camp for the night.	
	28/3/17	8 am	Left No 2 Rest Camp.	
		12.30 pm	Entrained at Havre.	
			Ad. Ars. 2/7	

J. Greenwood. Lieut.
Comnd. 197 Light Trench Mortar Battery

197th Brigade

66th Division.

197th LIGHT TRENCH MORTAR BATTERY MARCH 1917.

Army Form C. 2118.

Volume II
Confidential WAR DIARY of 19th L.T.M. Battery
INTELLIGENCE SUMMARY.
From 1/3 to 31/3/17

(Erase heading not required.)

Place	Date	Hour	Summary of Events and Information	Remarks and references to Appendices
Thiennes	1/3/17	6.30pm	Arrived. March to village of BOESEGHEM.	
Boeseghem	1/3/17	8.30pm	Arrived. Billeted in barns.	
	2/3/17	9am	Formed Hd Qrs & instructed battery	
	3/3/17	9am	Drilled Battery	
	6/3/17	6.30pm	Orders for move to LOCON received.	
	7/3/17	9am	Move for LOCON by route march.	
Locon	7/3/17	6pm	Arrived. Billeted in barns. Hd Qrs immediately established.	
	8/3/17	4.45pm	Orders for move to BETHUNE received.	
	9/3/17	11am	Moved to BETHUNE by march route.	
Bethune	9/3/17	12.30pm	Arrived, Hqrs established.	
	10/3/17	9am	1 Officer & 20 men reported from 2/5, 2/6, 2/7, 2/8 Bns Lancashire Fusiliers to be trained as reserves to Battery establishment	
	11/3/17	9am	Training & Reserves carried out	
	12/3/17	3.45pm	Orders for relief of 13th L.T.M. Battery received	
	13/3/17	3pm	Returned to whole of Reserves to Battery establishment	
	14/3/17	12 noon	Relief of 13 L.T.M.B. carried out. 1 + 2 sections 19 L.T.M.B. man in the line ride operation	
			(relief No 3.) Hd Qrs established	
Gorre	15/3/17	8am	Nothing to report	
	16/3/17	8am		
	17/3/17	8am		

Continued

Army Form C. 2118.

Volume II Continued
WAR DIARY
INTELLIGENCE SUMMARY.
(Erase heading not required.)

Instructions regarding War Diaries and Intelligence Summaries are contained in F. S. Regs., Part II. and the Staff Manual respectively. Title pages will be prepared in manuscript.

Place	Date	Hour	Summary of Events and Information	Remarks and references to Appendices
Gouy	18/3/17	8 am	Nothing to report.	
	19/3/17	8.30 am	Relief of 1 & 2 Sections 197 L.T.M.B. by 3 & 4 Sections. 1 man admitted to Hospital (with Septic Heel.)	
	20/3/17	8 am	Nothing to report.	
	21/3/17	8 am		
	22/3/17	8 am	Premature oozing gun burst, no damage to Personal.	
		8.30 am	Guns shelled by hostile artillery, no damage to Personal or equipment.	
	23/3/17	8 am	Relief of 3/4 Sections by 1/2 Sections.	
	24/3/17	8 am	Nothing to report.	
	25/3/17	8 am	— " —	
	26/3/17	8 am	— " —	
	27/3/17	8.30 am	Relief of 1/2 Sections by 3/4 Sections.	
	28/3/17	8 am	Nothing to report.	
	29/3/17	8 am		
	30/3/17	8 am		
	31/3/17	8.30 am	Relief of 3/4 Sections by 1/2 Sections.	

Greenwood Lieut
Commdg 197 L.T.M. Battery

197th Brigade.

66th Division.

197th LIGHT TRENCH MORTAR BATTERY APRIL 1917.

Volume III

Confidential

WAR DIARY

of 197 Light Trench Mortar Battery

INTELLIGENCE SUMMARY.

(Erase heading not required.) From 1/4/17 to 30/4/17

Army Form C. 2118.

Instructions regarding War Diaries and Intelligence Summaries are contained in F. S. Regs., Part II. and the Staff Manual respectively. Title pages will be prepared in manuscript.

Place	Date	Hour	Summary of Events and Information	Remarks and references to Appendices
Givenchy	1-4-17	8 am	Nothing to report.	
	2-4-17	2.30am	Hostile Artillery Bombarded Givenchy, no damage to Personnel.	
	3-4-17	8.30am	Relief of Sections 1 & 2 by Sections 3 & 4.	
		11 am	Hostile Artillery shelled Givenchy, no damage to Personnel.	
	4-4-17	3 pm	Hostile Artillery bombarded Givenchy, no damage to Personnel.	
	5-4-17	8 am	Nothing to report.	
	6-4-17			
	7-4-17	7.30pm	Relief of Sections 3 & 4 by Sections 1 & 2.	
	8-4-17	6 pm	Enemy shelled our emplacements with T. Mortar. One man killed by shell shock.	
	9-4-17		Nothing to report.	
	10-4-17	3.30pm	Hostile Artillery shelled our emplacements. No men killed by hostile shell.	
	11-4-17	8.30pm	Relief of Sections 1 & 2 by Sections 3 & 4. At 4.30pm Hostile Artillery bombarded Givenchy, no damage to Personnel.	
	12-4-17		Nothing to report.	
	13-4-17	8 am	Givenchy shelled by Hostile Artillery, no damage to Personnel.	
	14-4-17	12 am	Relief of Sections 3 & 4 by Sections 1 & 2. Also Hostile Bombardment on our emplacements, no men wounded.	
	15-4-17	8 am	Hostile Artillery active in Givenchy Sector.	
	16-4-17	2.30pm		
	17-4-17	8 am	Nothing to report.	
	18-4-17			
	19-4-17		Relief of Sections 1 & 2 by Sections 3 & 4. Staff Hostile bombardment at 4.30pm. Enemy shell burst our emplacement, wounded 4 men, killed 1 man	
	20-4-17	5-30pm	Rest Billet at Gorre, stayed in Hostile shell (two men killed + two wounded.)	
	22-4-17	8 am	Nothing to report.	
	23-4-17			
	24-4-17	8.30am	Relief of Sections 3 & 4 by Sections 1 & 2. Givenchy bombarded by Hostile Artillery, no damage to Personnel.	
	25-4-17	10 am	Light Signal sent to points F.3. a.y.6.	
	26-4-17	8 am	Nothing to report.	
	27-4-17			
	28-4-17	3 pm	Relief of Sections 1 & 2 by Sections 3 & 4. Givenchy shelled not damaged to Personnel. Our Stokes passing bombarded.	
	29-4-17	9 am	Hostile Trench Mortar bombarded our right front on 1st line	
			One man reported from JB J9 F20 to Rifles Quarters.	
	30-4-17	4 am	One man wounded from JB J9 F20 to Rifles Quarters.	

Givenchy 197 ~ 7.30 a.m. B.M. M.Y.
April 1917

Confidential

A.G.
3rd Echelon
Base.

Herewith Confidential War Diary Volume
III from 1-4-17 to 30-4-17 of the 197
Light Trench Mortar Battery.

A Greenwood Capt
Comdg 197 L.T.M. Battery.

197th Brigade.

66th Division.

197th LIGHT TRENCH MORTAR BATTERY MAY 1917.

66

Volume IV

Confidential

Army Form C. 2118.

WAR DIARY
of 197th Light Trench Mortar Battery.

INTELLIGENCE SUMMARY.

From 1/5/17 to 31/5/17

(Erase heading not required.)

Instructions regarding War Diaries and Intelligence Summaries are contained in F. S. Regs., Part II. and the Staff Manual respectively. Title pages will be prepared in manuscript.

Place	Date	Hour	Summary of Events and Information	Remarks and references to Appendices
Goose	1-5-17	8.30 am	Nothing to report.	
	2-5-17	8.30 am	Relief of Sections 3 & 4 by Sections 1 & 2. Our Stokes heavily bombarded SUNKEN ROAD Trench at 5pm. Hostile heavy artillery retaliated immediately and obtained direct hit on BUNNY HUTCH. Casualties 2 killed, 1 wounded, 1 shell shock.	
	3-5-17	8 am	Nothing to report.	
	4-5-17	5 pm	1 man reported from 3/6 Lan. Fus. to replace casualty.	
	5-5-17	8 am	Nothing to report.	
	6-5-17	8.30 am	Relief of Sections 1 & 2 by Sections 3 & 4. Our Stokes registered on enemy support lines. Hostile retaliation nil.	
	7-5-17	4 pm	Our Stokes bombarded CRATER TRENCH, "SUNKEN ROAD TRENCH". 1 man reported from 2/7 Lan. Fus. to replace casualty.	
	8-5-17	11.30 pm	(Our Stokes bombarded SUNKEN ROAD TRENCH. Hostile artillery very active but obtained no hits. [2 men reported from 2/7 Lan. Fus. to replace casualties.	
	9-5-17	8.30 am	Our Stokes bombarded CRATER TRENCH at intervals. Snipers fair damaged. Our Stokes put down a heavy barrage on enemy trenches on P. ESTUBERT Sector at 11.30 pm. Casualties 1 man wounded.	
	10-5-17	11.30 am	Relief of Sections 3 & 4 by Sections 1 & 2.	
	11-5-17	4.30 pm	Our Stokes bombarded area a.9.h. in conjunction with M.T.M. Enemy retaliated heavily but obtained no hits.	
	12-5-17	3 pm	Our Stokes bombarded area a.9.h. in conjunction with M.T.M.'s & artillery. Enemy retaliated but obtained no hits.	
	13-5-17	3.30 pm	1 man reported from 2/5 Lan. Fus. 1 man from 1/5 Lan. Bus to replace casualties.	
	14-5-17	8 am	Relief of Sections 1 & 2 by Sections 3 & 4. 1 man reported from 2/7 Lan. Fus. to replace casualty.	
	15-5-17	4.30 am	Our Stokes bombarded area a.9.h. in conjunction with M.T.M.'s & artillery. Enemy retaliation quiet.	
	16-5-17	11.30 am	Our Stokes bombarded SUNKEN ROAD Trench. Enemy retaliation quiet.	
	17-5-17	12.30 pm	Our Stokes bombarded SUNKEN ROAD Trench, C.T., CRATER Trench, "SUPPORT" trenches. Enemy retaliated but obtained no hits.	
	18-5-17	8 am	Relief of Sections 3 & 4 by Sections 1 & 2.	
	19-5-17	8 am	Nothing to report.	
	20-5-17	4.30 pm	Our Stokes active. Enemy retaliated. Last obtained no hits. 5 men from (cadre) 2/5th, 2/6th, 2/7th, 2/8th Lan. Fus attached for duty. 1 officer attached from 2/5th. 1 from 2/6th Lan. Fus.	
	21-5-17	2.30 pm	Our Stokes bombarded area a.9.d. Enemy retaliation weak. 1 man accidentally wounded.	
	22-5-17	8.30 am	Relief of Sections 1 & 2 by Sections 3 & 4. Enemy retaliated but obtained no hits.	
	23-5-17	11 am	Our Stokes bombarded area a.9.b. Our Stokes active.	
	24-5-17	10.30 am	Our Stokes active. Enemy retaliated briskly but obtained no hits.	
	25-5-17	10 am	Our Stokes bombarded a Advanced post in area a.9.d. Enemy retaliated heavily. 9 direct hit registered on SUNKEN ROAD. Gun out of action.	
	26-5-17	8.30 am	Relief of Sections 3 & 4 by Sections 1 & 2.	
	27-5-17	10.45 pm	GORRE bombarded by hostile artillery. No damage to personnel.	
	28-5-17	8.10 am	GORRE bombarded by hostile artillery. No damage to personnel.	
	29-5-17	11.30 am	Our Stokes carried out registering fire.	
	30-5-17	8 am	Relief of Sections 1 & 2 by Sections 3 & 4. Our Stokes active during the day. Enemy retaliated but obtained no hits.	
	31-5-17	6 am	Our Stokes bombarded area a.9.d. - PRUSSIAN WAY and area a.9.d. Enemy retaliation weak.	

Hqrs.
31-5-17

J. Greenwood Capt.
Commdg. 197 Light Trench Mortar Battery

A.5834 Wt: W.4973/M687 750,000 8/16 D, D. & L. Ltd. Forms/C.2118/13.

Secret.

D.A.G.
3rd Echelon

Herewith A.F. C2118 for this Unit for the month of May 1917.

Greenwood Capt
Comndg 197th L.T.M. Batty

In the Field
31/5/17

(stamp: 197TH LIGHT TRENCH MORTAR BATTERY Ref. No. S433 Date ......)

197th Brigade

66th Division

197th LIGHT TRENCH MORTAR BATTERY JUNE 1917.

Army Form C. 2118.

Volume V
Confidential
WAR DIARY
or
194th Right Trench Mortar Battery
INTELLIGENCE SUMMARY.
(Erase heading not required.)

From 1/6/17 to 30/6/17

Instructions regarding War Diaries and Intelligence Summaries are contained in F. S. Regs., Part II. and the Staff Manual respectively. Title pages will be prepared in manuscript.

Place	Date	Hour	Summary of Events and Information	Remarks and references to Appendices
Gorre.	1-6-17	11.30 AM	No Trench Mortar activity	
	2-6-17	11 AM	Our Stokes fired on area A9.b direct hits were obtained. Rect was on Trench Mortars by Capt. W. Moore Tucker.	
	3-6-17	9.30 AM	Relief 3 & 4 sections by 1 & 2 sections. Our stokes carried out a few registering shots with good results.	
	4-6-17	11.30 AM	During the morning our Stokes fired on SAXON WAY, PRUSSIAN WAY. Count A9.d 79.24 to A9.6 83.15 and Cater on the sandbag dump at hook H & I Sah. good shots were obtained and Trench Material was observed to be blown up. 1 man admitted to Hospital sick	
	5-6-17	12.30 PM	During the day our stokes registered and fired on SAXON WAY from point A9.d. 40.20 to A9.c. 14.40. Good results were obtained and Play Pistols retaliation took place.	
	6-6-17	6.30 PM	Our stokes registered and traversed. The enemys front line from point A9.b 65.82 to A9.b. 69.81. Trench material was thrown up in the explosion	
			Hostile retaliation comprising 4.2.5 was concentrated to the area of GIVENCHY CHURCH.	
	7-6-17	8.30 AM	Relief 1 & 2 sections by 3 & 4 sections. During the day, our stokes fired on area A9.b. 3 A9.d. Traversing fire was carried out from point A9.B. 12.50 to A9.b 70.04.	
			Good Rits were observed. Hostile retaliation consisted comprising 4, 2.3 & 9s. 2 men wounded	
	8-6-17	11.30 AM	During the day our stokes fired on A9.d 23.49. Direct hits were obtained	
	9-6-17	11.30 AM	H.Sah. and ambushed at A9.d 23.49. Traversing fire from point A9.b 23.12 to A9.d. P.M. Prussian Way, and hostile Machine Gun Emplacement. Sand bag dump, offshoots	
			at intervals throughout the day. our stokes registered the following points and traverses. Snipur post offshoot T. Sah. Sand bag dump offshoots H. Sah.	
			point A9.b. 80.15. to A9.d. 81.25. PRUSSIAN WAY. and A9.d 23.49. Direct Rits were obtained and damage was done. 1 Man returns from Hospital	
	10-6-17	10.30 NN	During the morning our stokes fired on the sand bag dump offshoots H.Sah. PRUSSIAN WAY, SAXON WAY and CRATER TRENCH great damage was done to these trenches	
			also retaliated to J. Hugo Boup and fired on Old means corner. At 8.57 P.M in co-operation with operations carried out by the Grenade on our right. Our stokes barraged SAXON WAY, & PRUSSIAN WAY Trenches. We	
	11-6-17	8 x 3 AM	Relief 3 & 4 sections by 1 & 2 sections. Our stokes fired on conducted working party.	
	12-6-17	5 x 30 PM	Our stokes fired in retaliation to the hostile Bombardment on the trenches of the Brigade on our left. we put down a Barrage at hook Canadian Orchard	
	13-6-17	3 AM	Our stokes bombarded the following strong points and Machine Gun Emplacements for an hour and a half with interval fire. A9.8.38.03. 33.23.30.35. and	
			S 29.A. 68.48. 28.99. Rates in 184. day our stokes fired on point A9.B. 54.50 & A9 62.12. with direct hits. 4 men slightly wounded 1 man whilst for duty	
	14-6-17	11.30 AM	Our stokes bombarded the enemy trenches from point A9.B.30.44 A9.6.41.50. Direct Rits were obtained	
	15-6-17	8.30 AM	Relief 1 & 2 sections by 3 & 4 sections. During the afternoon our stokes registered and fired behind Sandbag Dump offshoot H.Sah. Direct Rit were obtained	
			1 man reported for duty, 1 sent to Battery. 1 man admitted to Hospital	
	16-6-17	12.30	During the day our stokes fired on the Sandbag Dumps offshoot our Saps. Ye registered and fired on SAXON WAY, and PRUSSIAN WAY. Direct hits were	
			obtained on these targets. 1 man admitted to Hospital sick	
	17-6-17	6 P.M	Nothing to report	
	18-6-17	6 P.M	Our stokes ranged and fired on hostile dugout in MacAdam Trench	

Army Form C. 2118.

WAR DIARY Volume V Continued
or
INTELLIGENCE SUMMARY.
(Erase heading not required.)

Instructions regarding War Diaries and Intelligence Summaries are contained in F. S. Regs., Part II. and the Staff Manual respectively. Title pages will be prepared in manuscript.

Place	Date	Hour	Summary of Events and Information	Remarks and references to Appendices
Ghent	19-6-17	8.30 AM	Relief 3 & 4 sections by 1 & 2 sections	
"	20-6-17	3 P.m.	Relieved by 6" Siege R.T.M.B., 2 Officers and 2 NCOs staying with relieving Battery for 24 hours.	
"	21-6-17	12.15 AM	194. R.T.M.B. marched off from Billet to Rest Billet at point Y.M.C.2.6 (Belland Combined 2nd) . 2 Officers and 41 men attached to Battery returned to their units.	
Bellerive	22-6-17	11.30	Nothing to Report.	
"	23-6-17	7 AM	1 N.C.O. came with advance party. N.C.Os. and men Medically Examined.	
"	24-6-17	11 AM	Marched off from Rest Billet to Cloquez. Station where we entrained for Dunkerque. Hence to Billet at point H.11.6.5.b. (Belgium and France Sheet 19)	
"	25-6-17	9 AM	Training commenced	
"	26-6-17	9 AM	Nothing to report	
"	27-6-17	8 AM	COUDEKERQUE-BRANCHE was shelled to day by Hostile Naval Gun.	
"	28-6-17	9 AM	4 N.C.Os. and 40 men report for a 4 days course of Instruction on Trench Mortars.	
"	29-6-17	5 P.m.	Nothing to report.	
"	30-6-17	6 P.m.	" "	

Signed
30-6-17

Major O. Seager
Commanding 194 T.M.B.

197th Brigade.

66th Division.

197th LIGHT TRENCH MORTAR BATTERY JULY 1917.

CONFIDENTIAL

WAR DIARY

OF

197th. LIGHT TRENCH MORTAR BATTERY.

FROM 1st. JULY 1917 to 31st. JULY 1917.

(VOLUME 6.)

-:-:-:-:-:-:-:-:-:-:-:-:-:-

Volume VI

Confidential   Army Form C. 2118.

WAR DIARY
194. Right Trench Mortar Battery.
or
INTELLIGENCE SUMMARY.

(Erase heading not required.)   From 1/4/17 to 31/4/17

Instructions regarding War Diaries and Intelligence Summaries are contained in F.S. Regs., Part II. and the Staff Manual respectively. Title pages will be prepared in manuscript.

Place	Date	Hour	Summary of Events and Information	Remarks and references to Appendices
Coudekerque Branch	1-4-17	6 P.M	Nothing to Report.	
"	2-4-17	6 P.M	"	
"	3-4-17	6 P.M	"	
"	4-4-17	6 P.M	"	
"	5-4-17	3.30 P.M	H.M. King George visited XV Corps Area to day	
"	6-4-17	6 P.M	Nothing to Report	
"	7-4-17	3 A.M	4 N.C.O.s & 40 Men join their Batt. on completion of course on Trench Mortars. 2 Officers report for duty. 48 Men report for 7 days course of instruction on T.M.	
"	8-4-17	6 P.M	Nothing to Report	
Zuydcoote	9-4-17	10 A.M	Battery leave for New Area at Zuydcoote, Ferm Carton	
"	10-4-17	4 P.M	Nothing to Report	
"	11-4-17	"	"	
"	12-4-17	3 A.M	Battery leave for New Area in Coryde Les Bains	
Coxyde-Les-Bains	13-4-17	4 P.M	Nothing to Report	
"	14-4-17	"	"	
"	15-4-17	10 A.M	48 men rejoin Battn. on completion of T.M. course.	
"	16-4-17	8 P.M	Battery move to new area. Map Ref. R.32.A. (coud 1:52). 10 P.M. 1 & 2 Sub Sections relieve 2" R.T.M B on Newport Bains Sector	
Oost-Dunkerque	17-4-17	11 A.M	1 Man admitted to Hospital (sick).	
"	18-4-17	6 P.M	Nothing to Report	
"	19-4-17	6 P.M	"	
"	20-4-17	6 P.M	"	
"	21-4-17	4 P.M	3 & 4 Sections relieve 1 & 2 Sections	
"	22-4-17	6 P.M	Nothing to Report	
"	23-4-17	6 P.M	"	
"	24-4-17	6 P.M	"	
"	25-4-17	6 P.M	"	
"	26-4-17	3 P.M	T.R. R.T.M.B. were active to day on the enemies trench, from hand M.1.6.35.52 to M.1.6.55.40. Hostile artillery retaliation normal	
"	27-4-17	2.30 P.M	T.R. R.T. Mortars were active to day on Hostile trench on M.14.B. Hostile Retaliation normal.	
"	28-4-17	11 P.M	6 men wounded in action	
"	29-4-17	10 A.M	Battery move to New area Camp GABOR. 3 P.M. 194 R.T.M.B. relieved by 198 R.T.M.B. on Newport Bains Sector	
Coxyde	30-4-17	10 A.M	1 Officer & 1 Sgt. leave for a 18 days course of instruction on Trench Mortars at XV Corps. School	
"	31-4-17	10 P.M		

Hqrs In-the-field.
1-8-17.

Viscount
Capt.
Commdg. 194. R.T.M B

197th Brigade
66th Division.

197th LIGHT TRENCH MORTAR BATTERY AUGUST 1917.

Confidential

War Diary
of
194ᵗʰ Light Trench Mortar Battery.

From:- 1-8-17   To:- 31-8-17

(Volume VII.)

Army Form C. 2118.

WAR DIARY
VOLUME VII
INTELLIGENCE SUMMARY

of 194 Lgt Trench Mortar Battery

(Erase heading not required.)

From 1/8/14 to 31/8/14

Instructions regarding War Diaries and Intelligence Summaries are contained in F. S. Regs., Part II. and the Staff Manual respectively. Title pages will be prepared in manuscript.

Confidential

Place	Date	Hour	Summary of Events and Information	Remarks and references to Appendices
COXYDE BAINS	1-8-17	10-3pm	5 Men reported for duty with the Battery	
"	2-8-17	6-7pm	Nothing to report	
"	3-8-17	6-7pm	" " "	
"	4-8-17	3-3.30pm	1 Man reported for duty with the Battery	
"	5-8-17	6-7pm	Nothing to report	
"	6-8-17	6-7pm	" " "	
"	7-8-17	6-7pm	" " "	
"	8-8-17	4pm	1 Man reported for duty with the Battery	
"	9-8-17	9-9.30am	1 N.C.O. proceeded to Eng. course to Domninion Gun school	
"	10-8-17	6-7pm	Nothing to report	
"	11-8-17	6-7pm	" " "	
"	12-8-17	6-7pm	" " "	
"	13-8-17	5-6pm	" " "	
"	14-8-17	6-7pm	" " "	
"	15-8-17	10-10.30pm	2 N.C.O.s proceeded to XV Corps School of Inspection	
"	16-8-17	9-5pm	Men sent to hospital	
"	17-8-17	4.30pm	One officer & 2 ORs rejoined the Battery	Battery was in Reserve at
"	18-8-17	6pm	One officer proceeded to War Office on Commission course	weak camp. Sheller by hostile batteries
"	19-8-17	6pm	Nothing to report. Battery was shelled by hostile Batteries. No personnel injured	
"	"	4pm	Had returned to Battery from hospital	
"	20-8-17	6pm	Nothing to report	
OOST DUNKIRK	21-8-17	10pm	Battery moved to new gun stn in Gans Dunes 194 T.M.B. + relieved 199 T.M.B. Lieut Beach Sector	
"	22-8-17	3pm	The Battery engaged on Anti-aircraft shoots — required good shooting	
"	23-8-17	9-10am	Our stores arrived at Daterials during the day on the BARRICADE, the DIMPLE + BEACH AVENUE, shooting	
"	24-8-17	2-3.30pm	One man reported for duty with the Battery. Shells were active to-day on the BARRICADE, BEACH AVENUE	
"	25-8-17	9-9.30am	Good air observation that this meta observer life was exploded over scores fired at Dunkirk during the day, on the BARRICADE + BEACH WALK North recovered	
"	26-8-17	9-11am	Our shells fired during the day on BEACH AVENUE, and the BARRICADES with very good results	

A 5834 Wt. W4973/M687 750,000 8/16 D. D. & L. Ltd. Forms/C.2118/13.

Army Form C. 2118.

VOLUME VII CONTINUED
WAR DIARY
or
INTELLIGENCE SUMMARY.

(Erase heading not required.)

Instructions regarding War Diaries and Intelligence Summaries are contained in F. S. Regs., Part II. and the Staff Manual respectively. Title pages will be prepared in manuscript.

Place	Date	Hour	Summary of Events and Information	Remarks and references to Appendices
OOST DUNKERQUE	28-8-19	9 A.M	Our Stokes were active to-day on BEACH AVENUE. BACK WALK. 46.45 - 40.10 and THE BARRICADE. Trench material was thrown up in explosions.	
"	29-8-19	9.30 A.M	Our Stokes fired at intervals during the day on BEACH AVENUE. BEACH WALK and DUNE, the sand bags reported at M.14.b. 60 50 at 9 P.M. against this was concentrated on the whole of THE BARRICADE	
"	29-8-19	9.15 A.M.	Our Stokes during the day on BEACH WALK. BARRICADE, and BEACH AVENUE. M.14.b. Trench material was thrown up in explosions. Hostile retaliation Nil.	
"	30-8-19	5 A.M.	During the Day, Stokes fired on BARRICADE. BEACH AVENUE. BACK WALK, and the usual targets in area M.14.b. good results	
"	31-8-19	10 A.M.	During the day our Stokes fired on targets in M.14.b. and retaliation was Normal. Following him to mentioned in Divisional Progress Summary No 65" with good results also humans was seen to rise in the air The suspected O.P. in File Barricade at M.14.b. 60,30. the point immediately in front of the PIMPLE, where smoke was seen hostile retaliation Nil.	

Lt [signature]
In the field
31-8-19.

[signature] Capt
Commdg. 197. L.T.M.B

197th Brigade.

66th Division.

197th LIGHT TRENCH MORTAR BATTERY SEPTEMBER 1917.

ORIGINAL

CONFIDENTIAL.

WAR DIARY

of

197th. LIGHT TRENCH MORTAR BATTERY.

From :- 1st. September 1917.   To :- 30th. September 1917.

(V O L U M E 8).

****

Confidential

Army Form C. 2118.

VOLUME VIII
WAR DIARY
or
INTELLIGENCE SUMMARY

(Erase heading not required.)

197th Light Trench Mortar Battery

From 1/9/17 to 30/9/17.

Instructions regarding War Diaries and Intelligence Summaries are contained in F.S. Regs., Part II. and the Staff Manual respectively. Title pages will be prepared in manuscript.

Place	Date	Hour	Summary of Events and Information	Remarks and references to Appendices
COXYDE BAINS	1.9.17	11.A.M	12 Men reported for Duty with the Battery. Hostile Batteries shelled the Camp from 9 A.M. to 4 P.M. No personnel injured, at intervals during the day our Stokes carried out with good results. Traversing the BARRICADES.	
"	2.9.17	6 P.M.	Targets shot at during the day. BARRICADE, and near of BARRICADE. M.G. at M.14.6.05-40. BEACH AVENUE, and enemy post at M.14.6.20-30.	
"	3.9.17	6 P.M.	Our Stokes were active to-day on the following points were obtained, and several material thrown up in explosions, traversing the BARRICADE.	
"	4.9.17	6 P.M.	M.14.6.15-35 to M.14.6.30-54. TUNNEL ENTRANCE at M.14.6.25-25 and BARRICADE. Stokes were active today on the mentioned targets good hits were obtained. BEACH AVENUE. 60 shells were used up in the enemy. No personnel injured	
"	5.9.17	7.30 A.M	1. N.C.O proceeded at a course of Instruction at Ky Corps School Le Panne.	
"	6.9.17	9.30 A.M	Battery moved to a new area.	
"	"	10 P.M	1 Enemy Aeroplane dropped 10 Bombs in camp. No personnel injured.	
"	7.9.17	6 P.M.	Hostile Battery shelled the camp during the day. No personnel injured.	
"	8.9.17	2.30 P.M.	Battery retaliated against Typhoice.	
"	9.9.17	6 P.M.	Nothing to report.	
"	10.9.17	6 P.M.	2 Lt. Ott. attached to Battery for a course of Instruction.	
"	11.9.17	6 P.M.	1 Non returned to his Battalion.	
"	12.9.17	6 P.M.	Battery in special training. Firing line ammunition.	
"	13.9.17	6 P.M.	Enemy shelled the Battery camp during night of 12th & 13th.	
"	14.9.17	6 P.M.	Nothing to report.	
"	15.9.17	" "	do	
"	16.9.17	6 P.M.	Enemy aeroplane dropped two Bombs in Nr Battery camp. No personnel injured	
"	17.9.17	6 P.M.	Nothing to report	

Army Form C. 2118.

VOLUME VIII CONT'D
WAR DIARY
INTELLIGENCE SUMMARY.

(Erase heading not required.)

Instructions regarding War Diaries and Intelligence Summaries are contained in F. S. Regs., Part II. and the Staff Manual respectively. Title pages will be prepared in manuscript.

Place	Date	Hour	Summary of Events and Information	Remarks and references to Appendices
COXYDE BAINS	18.9.17	7 A.M.	1 Officer proceeded on leave to England	
"	19.9.17	6 p.m.	Nothing to report	
"	20.9.17	10 p.m.	Battery moved to new camp COXYDE BAINS.	
"	21.9.17	10 A.M.	Officers and N.C.Os. proceeded on a Course of Instruction at XV Corps School La Panne	
"	22.9.17	6 p.m.	Nothing to report	
"	23.9.17	3.30 p.m.	O.Rs. Returned to units after completing 14 days course of Instruction.	
"	24.9.17	10 A.M.	Battery moved to new area BRAY DUNES.	
BRAY DUNES	25.9.17	6 p.m.	Nothing to report	
"	26.9.17	8.34 p.m.	Enemy aeroplane dropped 3 Bombs on Battery's camp. 4 O.Rs. wounded.	
"	27.9.17	11.A.M.	Battery move to new area, conveyed by Motor Bus. NR VUB.	
ARQUES	28.9.17	6 p.m.	Nothing to report	
"	29.9.17	8 A.M.	Battery taking part in general Brigade training	
"	30.9.17	10 p.m.	Enemy aircraft dropped 4 Bombs among the enemy. No personnel injured.	

In the Field.
30.9.17

[signature]
COMMDG. 194 W. B. M. B.

197th Brigade.

66th Division.

197th LIGHT TRENCH MORTAR BATTERY OCTOBER 1917.

Volume IX

WAR DIARY
or
INTELLIGENCE SUMMARY

Army Form C. 2118.

Confidential

19th Light Trench Mortar Battery

From 1/10/17 to 31/10/17

Place	Date	Hour	Summary of Events and Information	Remarks and references to Appendices
ARQUES	1-10-17	Night 9 A.M	Enemy Aeroplanes dropped 9 Bombs, near Batterys billet, no personnel injured.	
"	2-10-17	9 A.M	Battery moved to new area.	
EECKE	3-10-17	7 A.M.	13 O.Rs. sent to Reinforcement Camp.	
"	4-10-17	10 A.M.	Battery moved to new area.	
WINNEZEELE	5-10-17	9 A.M	Nl9.a. Area. Battery moved to new area.	
YPRES	6-10-17	Night 9.6 A.M	Enemy Aeroplanes dropped 19 Bombs around and near Batterys Rug-outs, no personnel injured.	
"	7-10-17	8 A.M	Hostile Artillery slightly shelled Batterys area.	
"	8-10-17	3 P.M	Battery preparing for offensive operations. Battery went into action during the night.	
"	9-10-17	3.30 A.M 10 A.M	Battery co-operating with Battalions of Brigade in action in attack on PASSCHENDAELE RIDGE	
"	10-10-17	6 P.M	Battery in action for 12 metres. Battery came out of action. Casualties slight.	
"	11-10-17	7 P.M	Battery moved to new area, conveyed to destination by Motor Bus.	
WINNEZEELE	12-10-17	6 A.M	Nothing to report.	
"	13-10-17	8 A.M	Reinforcements from Reinforcement camp rejoined Battery.	
"	14-10-17	9 A.M	1 Officer and 1 O.R. proceeded to II ANZAC Corps School for 14 days course of Instruction.	
"	15-10-17	6 P.M	Nothing to report.	
"	16-10-17	6 P.M	" "	
"	17-10-17	6 P.M	" "	
"	18-10-17	6 P.M	" "	
"	19-10-17	2 P.M	2 Officers attended II ANZAC Corps School for a demonstration on the new Sling "Invincible" for "3" Stokes Mortar for use in offensive operations, and the Sling principle is being adopted. 1 O.R. admitted to Hospital.	
"	20-10-17	9 A.M	Battery moved to new area.	
RENESCURE	21-10-17	6 P.M	Nothing to Report.	
"	22-10-17	6 P.M		
"	23-10-17		Battery drew Ammunition for Special Brigade Training.	

Army Form C. 2118.

VOLUME IX CONT'D
WAR DIARY
or
INTELLIGENCE SUMMARY.
(Erase heading not required.)

Instructions regarding War Diaries and Intelligence Summaries are contained in F. S. Regs., Part II. and the Staff Manual respectively. Title pages will be prepared in manuscript.

Place	Date	Hour	Summary of Events and Information	Remarks and references to Appendices
RENESCURE	24-10-17	11 A.M	Battery carried out Dummy firing with very good results using new sling principle.	
"	25-10-17	10 A.M	Battery made up to Strength. B. O. Rs. of Battery gained Military Medal for past action.	
"	26-10-17	11 A.M	Battery fired Dummy Shells in practice for Special Brigade Training.	
"	27-10-17	8 A.M	Battery taking in Brigade Tactical Exercise with Live Ammunition.	
"	28-10-17	11 A.M	Battery carried out Dummy firing with slings.	
"	28-10-17	6 pm	Nothing to Report.	
"	29-10-17	9 A.M	Battery Inspected by F.M. Sir Douglas Haig. Ear.l. during a tour of Divisional Inspection.	
"	30-10-17	10 A.M	Battery carried out Dummy firing with slings, good results were obtained.	
"	31-10-17	8 A.M	Battery taking part in Brigade Tactical Exercise.	

In-the-Field
31-10-17

Rennie Lt
Comm'dg 194/6 F.M.B.

197th Brigade.

66th Division

----- ------

197th LIGHT TRENCH MORTAR BATTERY NOVEMBER 1917.

Confidential

War Diary

of

197th Light Trench Mortar Battery

From 1-11-17   To 30-11-17

Volume I

Army Form C. 2118.

VOLUME X
WAR DIARY
or
INTELLIGENCE SUMMARY
(Erase heading not required.)

Confidential

194th Light Trench Mortar Battery.
from 1/11/17 to 30/11/17

Instructions regarding War Diaries and Intelligence Summaries are contained in F.S. Regs., Part II. and the Staff Manual respectively. Title pages will be prepared in manuscript.

Place	Date	Hour	Summary of Events and Information	Remarks and references to Appendices
RENESCURE	1-11-17	8 A.M	Battery in compliance with Brigade Training Programme. Route March with Battalion.	
"	2-11-17	8 A.M	Battery took part in Brigade Tactical Exercise.	
"	3-11-17	3 P.M	Battery on Training. Dummy firing with Slings.	
"	4-11-17	6 P.M	Nothing to report.	
"	5-11-17	9 A.M	Battery with the Battalion on a Route March.	
"	6-11-17	8 A.M	Battery taking part in Brigade Tactical Exercise.	
"	7-11-17	6 P.M	Nothing to report.	
"	8-11-17	9 A.M	Battery moved to new area.	
WESTOUTRE	9-11-17	10 A.M	Battery moved to new area.	
YPRES	10-11-17	10 A.M	Battery moved up to the line.	
ZONEBEKE (SECTOR)	11-11-17	3-30 P.M	Enemy Artillery heavily shelled Battery Hq.rs.	
"	12-11-17	10 A.M	No Trench Mortar activity.	
"	13-11-17	5 A.M	Enemy heavily shelled area with Gas Shells, Enemy aeroplane dropped 2 Bombs near Battery Hq.rs. 1 personnel injured	
"	14-11-17	10 A.M	Enemy Aeroplane dropped 2 Bombs on Battery H.P. No Trench Mortar activity.	
"	15-11-17	5 P.M	No Trench Mortar activity.	
"	16-11-17	3-0 P.M	Battery H.P. area subjected to heavy bombardment with Gas Shells.	
"	17-11-17	4 P.M	No Trench Mortar activity.	
"	18-11-17	3-30 P.M	No Trench Mortar activity.	
"	19-11-17	2-0 P.M	Battery relieved in the line, and moved to new area.	
YPRES	20-11-17	11-0 A.M	Battery moved to new area.	
DICKEBUSCH	21-11-17	10 A.M	Battery thoroughly cleaning up from last action.	
"	22-11-17	7 A.M	Battery moved to new area, O.R. departed to England on leave. Battery conveyed to destination by Motor Bus.	
STAPLE	23-11-17	6 P.M	Nothing to report.	
"	24-11-17	9 A.M	Battery on Steady Training.	
"	25-11-17	9 A.M	Battery on Training as in Syllabus of Training submitted to Bde. Hq.rs.	
"	26-11-17	10-0 A.M	102 reported for duty with Battery	
"	27-11-17	10-0 A.M	1 O.R. reported for duty with the Battery	
"	28-11-17	7-0 A.M	Battery in conjunction with Programme submitted to Bde Hq.rs. in steady training	
"	29-11-17	8-30 P.M	1 O.R. returned to battery from hospital.	
"	30-11-17			

In the Field.
30-11-17

J. Edward Lavinchers Lt
Commdg. 194th L.T.M.B.

197th Brigade.
66th Division.

197th LIGHT TRENCH MORTAR BATTERY DECEMBER 1917.

Confidential

War Diary

of

197th Light Trench Mortar Battery

From: 1-12-17   To: 31-12-17

Volume XI

Army Form C. 2118.

VOLUME XI
WAR DIARY
or
INTELLIGENCE SUMMARY.

197th Light Trench Mortar Battery

(Erase heading not required.)

Instructions regarding War Diaries and Intelligence Summaries are contained in F. S. Regs., Part II. and the Staff Manual respectively. Title pages will be prepared in manuscript.

Confidential

Place	Date	Hour	Summary of Events and Information	Remarks and references to Appendices
STAPLE	1-12-17	10 AM	Battery as in "Syllabus of Training" submitted to Bde Hqrs. in Steady Training	
"	2-12-17	6 PM	Nothing to Report.	
"	3-12-17	11 AM	Battery having a New Gun Drill.	
"	4-12-17	6 PM	2 ORs Reported for Duty with Battery.	
"	5-12-17	9 AM	Battery in Training Route March.	
"	6-12-17	3 PM	Battery on Training, practising Anti-aircraft firing.	
"	7-12-17	3 PM	Battery on Route March with Battalion. 1 Officer returned from Leave.	
"	8-12-17	6 PM	Nothing to Report.	
"	9-12-17	11 AM	Battery in Training, carrying out Anti aircraft Firing.	
"	10-12-17	9 AM	Battery Route March.	
"	11-12-17	9 AM	1 OR. proceeded on a Course of Instruction on "Physical Training and Bayonet Fighting" at the Anzac School.	
"	12-12-17	6 PM	Nothing to Report.	
"	13-12-17	8.30 AM	Battery in Training Route March with Battalion.	
"	14-12-17	6 PM	Nothing to Report.	
"	15-12-17	11 AM	Battery in Training. 1 OR proceeded on a Course of Instruction at Anzac School.	
"	16-12-17	11 AM	Battery Dummy Firing on Range.	
"	17-12-17	11 AM	Battery Firing Smoke Bombs. 1 Officer proceeded to England on Leave.	
"	18-12-17	9 AM	Battery Route March.	
"	19-12-17	3 PM	Christmas Day Festivities held. practising a "Smoke Barrage".	
"	20-12-17	10 AM	Battery in Training, Firing Smoke Bombs.	
"	21-12-17	4 PM	1 Officer returned from Leave.	
"	22-12-17	11 AM	Battery on Dummy Firing	
"	23-12-17	10 AM	Nothing to Report.	
"	24-12-17	10 AM	Battery on Dummy Firing	
"	25-12-17	8 AM	Church & Kit Parade	
"	26-12-17	11 AM	Christmas Day. General Parade.	
"	27-12-17	9 AM	Battery Dummy Firing on Range	
"	28-12-17	11 AM	1 OFF. and 1 OR proceeded to England on Leave.	
"	29-12-17	6 PM	Battery in Training Firing Smoke Bombs.	
"	30-12-17	5 PM	Nothing to Report. Smoke Bombs.	
"	31-12-17	10 AM	1 Officer reported for Duty with Battery. Battery in Training, Firing Dummy Ammunition on Range.	

In the Field
31-12-17

Commdg. 197 L.T.M.B. Capt

197ᵗʰ I.B.

Brigade Trench Mortar

Jan 1918

Army Form C. 2118.

WAR DIARY
or
INTELLIGENCE SUMMARY.
(Erase heading not required.)

1916 JAN

Place	Date	Hour	Summary of Events and Information	Remarks and references to Appendices
STAPLE	1		Battery in Training	
"	2		Battery in Training and doing agricultural work in Bulle area	
"	3		- do - Dummy firing	
"	4		- do -	
"	5		- do -	
"	6		- do -	
"	7		- do -	
"	8		- do -	
"	9		- do -	
"	10		- do -	
MORBECQUE	11		Battery proceeded to 25th Corps T.M. School for training	
"	12		Battery in Training	
"	13		- do -	
"	14		- do -	
HALIFAX	15		Battery rejoined Brigade Group in Halifax	

WAR DIARY
or
INTELLIGENCE SUMMARY.

Army Form C. 2118.

Place	Date	Hour	Summary of Events and Information	Remarks and references to Appendices
HALIFAX AREA	16		Battery relieved 198 T.M. Batty in line Passchendaele Sector	
YPRES	17		Battery in Line. S.O.S and A.A. work	
	18		to	
	19		to	
	20		to	
	21		to	
	22		to	
	23		to	
	24		to	
	25		to	
	26		Battery in action against enemy aircraft	
	27		Battery in Line	
HALIFAX AREA	28		Battery relieved by 99 T.M. Batty, then proceeded to Hilda Halifax area	
	29		Battery training and equipping	
	30		to	
	31		to	

Army Form C. 2118.

WAR DIARY
or
INTELLIGENCE SUMMARY.
(Erase heading not required.)

Instructions regarding War Diaries and Intelligence Summaries are contained in F. S. Regs., Part II. and the Staff Manual respectively. Title pages will be prepared in manuscript.

Place	Date	Hour	Summary of Events and Information	Remarks and references to Appendices
HALIFAX AREA	1		Battery in Training	
	2		do	
YPRES	3		Battery relieved 196 T.M.Btty in line	
"	4		Battery in Line	
"	5		do	
"	6		do	
"	7		do	
"	8		Battery relieved by 1st New Zealand T.M.Bty.	
HALIFAX AREA	9		Battery in Training	
ST JAN TER BRZEGE	10		Battery moved to new Area Rest Camp	
"	11		Battery in Training	
"	12		do	
"	13		do	
"	14		do	
"	15		do	
MARCELCAVE	16		Battery moved to new Area	

Coombes. Captain

Army Form C. 2118.

WAR DIARY
or
INTELLIGENCE SUMMARY.
(Erase heading not required.)

Instructions regarding War Diaries and Intelligence Summaries are contained in F. S. Regs., Part II. and the Staff Manual respectively. Title pages will be prepared in manuscript.

Place	Date	Hour	Summary of Events and Information	Remarks and references to Appendices
MARCELCAVE	17		Battery in Training	
	18		do	
	19		do	
	20		do	
	21		do	
	22		do	
	23		do	
	24		do	
	25		Battery cooperating in Brigade Tactical Scheme	
	26		Battery in Training	
	27		do	
VILLERS CARBONNEL	28		Battery moved to new Area	

M. Crombie Captain

CONFIDENTIAL

WAR DIARY
OF

197th L.T.M. Battery

from Feby 1st to Feby 28th 1918.

CONFIDENTIAL.

WAR DIARY

OF

197th L. T. M. BATTERY.

From 1st. September 1918 to 30th September 1918.

Army Form C. 2118.

197th T.M. Battery
September 1918.

WAR DIARY
or
INTELLIGENCE SUMMARY.
(Erase heading not required.)

Place	Date	Hour	Summary of Events and Information	Remarks and references to Appendices
BERNEVAL-LE-GRAND.	1/9/18		The Battery carried out training at the 66th Divnl. Light Trench Mortar School.	
	10/9/18		Personnel of the 64th Royal Dublin Fusiliers were transferred from 197th to 195th L.T.M.B.	
ABANCOURT.	16/9/18		Battery left the 66th Divnl. L.T.M. School, proceeding by motor lorry convoy to ABANCOURT camp. The personnel of the 18th (L.M.Y.) Bn. The King's Liverpool Regt. including CAPT. J.F. JAGOE, officer commanding the Battery, were transferred to 199th L.T.M.B. Lieut. W.S.R. STROYAN, 10th Black Watch, took over command. Personnel were composed of 15 O.R. of 10th Black Watch, but 48 O.R. from this battalion were attached for duty.	
HAUDRICOURT.	19/9/18		Battery moved from ABANCOURT to HAUDRICOURT.	
	21/9/18		Lieut. R.W. DICKSON, 2/Lieut. H.G. GYLE, 2/Lieut. Q. ANDERSON, 10th Black Watch, were attached for duty. Lieut. R.W. DICKSON took over command from this date.	
	23/9/18		Training of new personnel commenced.	
	27/9/18		Lieut. L.S.R. STROYAN and 2/Lieut. T. CARSON (10th Black Watch) on the strength of this battalion were struck off the effective strength of the Battery.	

Regl. reshuffle having been taken on the strength of this battalion.

R.W. Dickson, Lieut.
Comdg. 197th L.T.M.B.

www.ingramcontent.com/pod-product-compliance
Lightning Source LLC
Chambersburg PA
CBHW081457160426
43193CB00013B/2510